# SUNDAY MEALTIME PRAYERS

Michael Kwatera, O.S.B.

*A Liturgical Press Book*

THE LITURGICAL PRESS
Collegeville, Minnesota

*For*
*Dave, Micki, Chris, Mike, and Katie:*
*I thank my God for you.*

# CONTENTS

## EASTER SEASON

## ORDINARY TIME II

## ORDINARY TIME III

# PREFACE

Although recommended to laypersons by the Second Vatican Council, the Liturgy of the Hours (formerly called the Divine Office) has remained a largely unfamiliar and untried form of daily prayer for many Christians.[1] Nearly twenty-five years ago, authors like William G. Storey and Gabe Huck suggested how Evening Prayer might be combined with the evening meal.[2] They proposed the following order for the traditional elements of Evening Prayer:

- brief light service celebrating Christ, the Light of the World
- an evening psalm (Psalm 140/141 or another psalm)
- sharing of the meal
- a Scripture reading
- the Gospel canticle (the *Magnificat* of the Blessed Virgin Mary, Luke 1:46-55)
- prayers of intercession
- the Lord's Prayer and a blessing

This book is an attempt to let such prayer "frame" the family's midday brunch or evening meal on the Lord's Day.

According to a report on National Public Radio, there is not even *one* meal taken in common by most families each day. But there is some evidence that Sunday remains a special day in Christian consciousness and practice, a day for special time together and for special meals (I remember how, when I was a child, my mother marked Sunday with a dessert of frozen strawberries at dinner). Why shouldn't

Sunday be a special time for family prayer, especially around a meal on that day? But the prayers in this book might well be used on days other than Sunday.

The sets of prayers are arranged according to the seasons of the liturgical year, beginning with Advent. The two provided forms (1 and 2) can be alternated for the sake of variety. Some Sundays have proper prayers (for example, Holy Family, Epiphany, Passion [Palm] Sunday, and Easter Sunday). The Scripture readings are taken from the *Contemporary English Version* (American Bible Society, 1991). The psalms are taken from the Liturgical Psalter published by the International Commission on English in the Liturgy (ICEL, 1994), and from the *Contemporary English Version,* and are labeled accordingly. This latter version, which is used in the Roman Catholic *Lectionary for Masses with Children,* can be read and understood easily by people of all ages. The psalms, which are the common responsorial psalms for seasonal use in the *Lectionary for Mass,* have been divided into parts for a soloist and all; the use of the *Contemporary English Version* and the ICEL version will make it easy for children to speak the solo parts in the psalms. After each psalm, a prayer based on the psalm asks God's blessing on the meal and on those who share it.

Texts of Scripture readings are provided, but others might be chosen and read from the family Bible. During the intercessions families might wish to offer their own petitions in place of or in addition to the ones included.

There are many reasons why families are finding it difficult to pray together: few members are at home regularly; they are busy with meetings, overtime, activities, events, athletic practices and games, entertainment, school and classes, shopping; they do not know how to pray; they are embarrassed to be seen taking time to pray. Yet "after a busy day, a family needs time for silence and reflection; for forgiveness; for encouragement and strength; for satisfaction over good things; for praising and thanking God; for sharing with one another; for asking God's help for themselves and others."[3] The prayers in this book, offered for Sunday mealtimes, can provide for these needs after a busy weekend. When used at the evening meal on Sunday, these prayers can enable a family to end this holy day by giving thanks for God's gifts of time and nourishment.

November 1, 1995                                    Michael Kwatera, O.S.B.
Solemnity of All Saints

## NOTES

[1] "Pastors should see to it that the chief hours, especially vespers, are celebrated in common in church on Sundays and the more solemn feasts. The laity, too, are encouraged to recite the divine office either with the priests, or among themselves, or even individually" *Sacrosanctum concilium* (Constitution on the Sacred Liturgy) 100.

[2] William Storey, "The Hours for the People," *Liturgy* 18, no. 5 (May 1973) 7; Gabe Huck, *A Book of Family Prayer* (New York: Seabury, 1979) 37.

[3] "Helping Families to Pray," *National Bulletin on Liturgy* 14, no. 80 (September–October 1981) 166.

# ADVENT

## FORM 1
*First and Third Sundays of Advent*

**LIGHT SERVICE**

*After lighting the candle(s) on the table or on the Advent wreath:*

**Leader:** Jesus Christ is the light of the world.

**All:** A LIGHT NO DARKNESS CAN OVERCOME.

*or*

**Leader:** Light and peace in Jesus Christ our Lord.

**All:** THANKS BE TO GOD.

*Psalm 25:4-5abc, 8-9, 10 and 14 (CEV)*

**Solo:** To you, O Lord, I lift my soul.

**All:** Show me your paths
and teach me to follow;
guide me by your truth
and instruct me.
You keep me safe.

**Solo:** You are honest and merciful,
and you teach sinners
how to follow your path.
You lead humble people
to do what is right
and to stay on your path.

5

**All:**        Glory to the Father, and to the Son,
and to the Holy Spirit:
as it was in the beginning, is now,
and will be for ever. Amen.

**Leader:**  Let us pray.

*Pause for silent prayer.*

Lord God,
bless this table
and let the food we share
strengthen us in your service.
We ask this through Jesus Christ,
who comes in your name
and keeps us safe,
for ever and ever.

**All:**        AMEN.

## SHARING OF THE MEAL

*After the dishes are cleared away:*

## SCRIPTURE READING        *Philippians 4:4-7*

A reading from the Letter of Paul to the Philippians

Always be glad because of the Lord! I will say it again: Be glad. Always be gentle with others. The Lord will soon be here. Don't worry about anything, but pray about everything. With thankful hearts offer up your prayers and requests to God. Then, because you belong to Christ Jesus, God will bless you with peace that no one can completely understand. And this peace will control the way you think and feel.

**Reader:**  The word of the Lord.

**All:**        THANKS BE TO GOD.

## SILENT REFLECTION

## RESPONSE TO THE READING

**Leader:** Lord, let your face shine upon us
and we shall be saved.

**All:** LORD, GOD OF HOSTS,
COME AND SET US FREE.

## INTERCESSIONS

**Leader:** Lord Jesus, master of all times and seasons, we
ask you to fill these Advent days of waiting with
your saving love. Hear us as we pray: COME,
LORD JESUS.

• That the leaders of the Church will know your coming as
they promote unity among Christians, we pray:

• That the leaders of nations will know your coming as they
work to end oppression and violence, we pray:

• That the unemployed will know your coming as they find
opportunities for fruitful work, we pray:

• That the sick will know your coming as they receive the
kindness of their sisters and brothers, we pray:

• That the dead will know your coming as they rise to everlasting life in your presence, we pray:

As we prepare to welcome Christ now and at the end of time,
let us pray as he taught us: Our Father . . . .

## BLESSING

**Leader:** May the God of peace make us perfect and holy,
and may we be safe and blameless, spirit, soul,
and body, for the coming of our Lord Jesus Christ.

**All:** AMEN.

*A sign of peace may be exchanged.*

# FORM 2
*Second and Fourth Sundays of Advent*

## LIGHT SERVICE

*After lighting the candle(s) on the table or on the Advent wreath:*

**Leader:** Jesus Christ is the light of the world.

**All:** A LIGHT NO DARKNESS CAN OVERCOME.

*or*

**Leader:** Light and peace in Jesus Christ our Lord.

**All:** THANKS BE TO GOD.

*Psalm 85:8-9, 10-11, 12-13 (CEV)*

**Solo:** I will listen to you, LORD God,
because you promise peace
to those who are faithful
and no longer foolish.
You are ready to rescue
everyone who worships you,
so that you will live with us
in all of your glory.

**All:** Love and loyalty
will come together;
goodness and peace will unite.
Loyalty will sprout
from the ground;
justice will look down
from the sky above.

**Solo:** Our LORD, you will bless us;
our land will produce
wonderful crops.
Justice will march in front,
making a path
for you to follow.

**All:**     Glory to the Father, and to the Son,
and to the Holy Spirit:
as it was in the beginning, is now,
and will be for ever. Amen.

**Leader:** Let us pray.

*Pause for silent prayer.*

Saving God, bless the food we are about to eat,
and bless the cooks *(name them)*
who have labored to prepare it.
Make us eager to welcome the One
in whom your goodness and peace unite,
Jesus Christ, our Lord.

**All:**     AMEN.

## SHARING OF THE MEAL

*After the dishes are cleared away:*

## SCRIPTURE READING                    *James 5:7-9*

A reading from the Letter of James

My friends, be patient until the Lord returns. Think of farmers who wait patiently for the spring and summer rains to make their valuable crops grow. Be patient like those farmers and don't give up. The Lord will soon be here! Don't grumble about each other or you will be judged, and the judge is right outside the door.

**Reader:** The word of the Lord.

**All:**     THANKS BE TO GOD.

## SILENT REFLECTION

## RESPONSE TO THE READING

**Leader:**  A herald's voice cries out in the desert:

**All:**  PREPARE THE WAY OF THE LORD;
MAKE STRAIGHT HIS PATHS.

## INTERCESSIONS

**Leader:**  The Lord Jesus is always near to us, always coming into our hearts. As we long to see Christ's glory at the end of the ages, let us ask the Father to hear us as we pray: LORD, BLESS YOUR PEOPLE.

• That the Lord will give wisdom to those who guide and teach the Church, we pray:

• That the Lord will give comfort to those who live in the agony of war, we pray:

• That the Lord will give healing to those who are weakened by sin and sickness, we pray:

• That the Lord will give perseverance to those who are persecuted for the truth, we pray:

• That the Lord will give hope to the dying who await the newness of eternal life, we pray:

Let us ask for the blessings of God's reign in the words Jesus gave us: Our Father . . . .

## BLESSING

**Leader:**  May we grow in the grace and knowledge of our Lord and Savior Jesus Christ, to whom be glory now and in the day of eternity.

**All:**  AMEN.

*A sign of peace may be exchanged.*

# CHRISTMAS SEASON

## HOLY FAMILY
*Sunday within the Octave of Christmas
or if Christmas falls on Sunday, December 30*


### LIGHT SERVICE

*After lighting the candle(s) on the table:*

**Leader:** Jesus Christ is the light of the world. Alleluia!

**All:** A LIGHT NO DARKNESS CAN OVERCOME.
ALLELUIA!

*or*

**Leader:** Light and peace in Jesus Christ our Lord. Alleluia!

**All:** THANKS BE TO GOD. ALLELUIA!

*Psalm 128:1, 2-4, 5-6* (ICEL)

**Solo:** How good to revere the Lord,
to walk in God's path.

**All:** Your table rich from labor—
how good for you!
Your beloved, a fruitful vine
in the warmth of your home.
Like olive shoots,
children surround your table.
This is your blessing
when you revere the Lord.

**Solo:** May the Lord bless you from Zion!
May you see Jerusalem prosper

11

every day of your life.
May you see your children's children,
and on Israel, peace!

**All:**  Glory to the Father, and to the Son,
and to the Holy Spirit:
as it was in the beginning, is now,
and will be for ever. Amen.

**Leader:**  Let us pray.

*Pause for silent prayer.*

God of our joy,
bless us
and the gifts
you have given us.
May our eating together
be a sign of the goodness and peace
you give to all people
in your Son,
Jesus Christ, the Lord.

**All:**  AMEN.

## SHARING OF THE MEAL

*After the dishes are cleared away:*

## SCRIPTURE READING                    *Colossians 3:12-15*

A reading from the Letter of Paul to the Colossians

God loves you and has chosen you as his special people. So
be gentle, kind, humble, meek, and patient. Put up with each
other, and forgive anyone who does you wrong, just as Christ
has forgiven you. Love is more important than anything else.
It is what ties everything completely together.

Each one of you is part of the body of Christ, and you were
chosen to live together in peace. So let the peace that comes
from Christ control your thoughts. And be grateful.

**Reader:** The word of the Lord.

**All:** THANKS BE TO GOD.

## SILENT REFLECTION

## RESPONSE TO THE READING

**Leader:** God sent the only Son into the world. Alleluia!

**All:** THE LOVE OF GOD SHONE FORTH AMONG US. ALLELUIA!

## INTERCESSIONS

**Leader:** Lord Jesus Christ, Son of Mary, pour out your grace on the whole human family and renew our lives as we celebrate your birth. Hear us as we pray: LORD, BE OUR LIFE AND SALVATION.

- For every family, that wives, husbands and children grow together in love and holiness:

- For people of all ages in life, that they honor and care for one another:

- For all children and for the defenseless, that they be shielded from harm in spirit, soul, and body:

- For young people whose lives are full of promise, that they meet the future with courage and confidence:

- For people in the prime of life, that their love and labor bring good to others and peace to themselves:

- For elderly people, that they be generous in heart and blessed with wisdom and strength:

- For those who are near death, that they be welcomed to the feast of eternal life:

As God's family, holy and beloved, let us pray to the Father as Jesus taught us: Our Father . . . .

## BLESSING

**Leader:** May the God of love, harmony, and peace be with us always.

**All:** AMEN.

*A sign of peace may be exchanged.*

## EPIPHANY
*Sunday between January 2 and January 8*

## LIGHT SERVICE

*After lighting the candle(s) on the table:*

**Leader:** Jesus Christ is the light of the world. Alleluia!

**All:** A LIGHT NO DARKNESS CAN OVERCOME. ALLELUIA!

*or*

**Leader:** Light and peace in Jesus Christ our Lord. Alleluia!

**All:** THANKS BE TO GOD. ALLELUIA!

*Psalm 98:1, 2-3, 4-6, 9 (ICEL)*

**Solo:** Sing to the Lord a new song,
the Lord of wonderful deeds.
Right hand and holy arm
brought victory to God.

**All:** God made that victory known,
revealed justice to nations,
remembered a merciful love
loyal to the house of Israel.
The ends of the earth have seen
the victory of our God.

**Solo:** Shout to the Lord, you earth,
break into song, into praise!
Sing praise to God with a harp,
with a harp and sound of music.
With sound of trumpet and horn,
shout to the Lord, our king.

**All:** The Lord our God comes,
comes to rule the earth,
justly to rule the world,
to govern the peoples aright.

**All:** Glory to the Father, and to the Son,
and to the Holy Spirit:
as it was in the beginning, is now,
and will be for ever. Amen.

**Leader:** Let us pray.

*Pause for silent prayer.*

All-powerful God,
visit this table
and renew the strength of us all.
May this food and this time together
be a sign of your merciful love,
through Christ our Lord.

**All:** AMEN.

## SHARING OF THE MEAL

*After the dishes are cleared away:*

## SCRIPTURE READING                    *Titus 2:11-14*

A reading from the Letter of Paul to Titus

God has shown us how kind he is by coming to save all
people. He taught us to give up our wicked ways and our
worldly desires and to live decent and honest lives in this
world. We are filled with hope, as we wait for the glorious

return of our great God and Savior Jesus Christ. He gave himself to rescue us from everything that is evil and to make our hearts pure. He wanted us to be his own people and to be eager to do right.

**Reader:** The word of the Lord.

**All:** THANKS BE TO GOD.

## SILENT REFLECTION

## RESPONSE TO THE READING

**Leader:** Salvation has been made known by the Lord. Alleluia!

**All:** ALL THE ENDS OF THE EARTH HAVE SEEN IT. ALLELUIA!

## INTERCESSIONS

**Leader:** Lord Jesus, though born a child, you reign as king. You have revealed in human flesh the marvelous love of our God for all people. Accept the homage we offer and hear us as we pray: LORD, THROUGH YOUR BIRTH, GIVE US LIFE.

• King of the Nations, you called the Magi to be the first of the Gentiles to kneel before you; gather people of every race, language, and way of life to praise you in your Church.

• Sun of Justice, you judge the peoples with fairness; free the oppressed and break the power of evil over human lives.

• Prince of Peace, you speak words of peace to the nations; shatter the weapons of war and give us peace from on high.

• Savior of the Poor, you defend the needy and the helpless; comfort sorrowing families, and protect all unborn children.

• Lord, you are blest for ever and endure like the sun; fulfill for the dead the glorious promise of your salvation and welcome them around your throne.

Let us pray to the Father as Jesus, the eternal King, has taught us: Our Father . . . .

## BLESSING

**Leader:** May the God of infinite goodness scatter the darkness of sin and brighten our hearts with holiness.

**All:** AMEN.

*A sign of peace may be exchanged.*

## BAPTISM OF THE LORD
*Sunday after January 6;*
*but where Epiphany has been transferred to a Sunday and*
*when it falls on January 7 or 8, the Baptism of the Lord*
*is celebrated on the following Monday*

## LIGHT SERVICE

*After lighting the candle(s) on the table:*

**Leader:** Jesus Christ is the light of the world. Alleluia!

**All:** A LIGHT NO DARKNESS CAN OVERCOME. ALLELUIA!

*or*

**Leader:** Light and peace in Jesus Christ our Lord. Alleluia!

**All:** THANKS BE TO GOD. ALLELUIA!

*Psalm 29:1-2, 3-4, 9-11* (ICEL)

**Solo:**    Give the Lord glory, you spirits!
Give glory! Honor God's strength!
Honor the name of the Lord!
Bow when the Lord comes,
majestic and holy.

**All:**    God's voice thunders
above the massive seas;
powerful, splendid.
All shout "Glory" in your temple, Lord.
For you rule the mighty waters,
you rule over all for ever.
Give strength to your people, Lord,
and bless your people with peace.

**All:**    Glory to the Father, and to the Son,
and to the Holy Spirit:
as it was in the beginning, is now,
and will be for ever. Amen.

**Leader:**    Let us pray.

*Pause for silent prayer.*

Lord our God,
bless the food we are about to eat
and look kindly
upon those who have prepared it:
*(name them).*
We ask this through your Son,
who out of the wonder of your love
lives in our midst,
now and for ever.

**All:**    AMEN.

## SHARING OF THE MEAL

*After the dishes are cleared away:*

**SCRIPTURE READING** *Acts 10:34-38*

A reading from the Acts of the Apostles

Peter said to Cornelius and his household: "Now I am certain that God treats all people alike. God is pleased with everyone who worships him and does right, no matter what nation they come from. This is the same message that God gave to the people of Israel, when he sent Jesus Christ, the Lord of all, to offer peace to them.

"You surely know what happened everywhere in Judea. It all began in Galilee after John had told everyone to be baptized. God gave the Holy Spirit and power to Jesus from Nazareth. He was with Jesus, as he went around doing good and healing everyone who was under the power of the devil."

**Reader:** The word of the Lord.

**All:** THANKS BE TO GOD.


**SILENT REFLECTION**


**RESPONSE TO THE READING**

**Leader:** Christ is the image of the invisible God. Alleluia!

**All:** HE IS THE FIRST-BORN OF ALL CREATION. ALLELUIA!


**INTERCESSIONS**

**Leader:** Lord Jesus, at your baptism you entered the Jordan River and made water a well brimming over with the Spirit of life. Through water and the Spirit, we become your holy people, called to service after the pattern of your own. Hear us as we pray: GRANT US YOUR SALVATION.

• Christ, revealed by your baptism as a light to the nations:

- Christ, proclaimed by your baptism as the Father's beloved Son:

- Christ, accepting by your baptism the saving vocation that God had prepared for you:

- Christ, sanctifying by your baptism all of creation:

- Christ, anointed by your baptism as the priest of the new covenant:

In the unity of the Holy Spirit, let us pray to the Father as the beloved Son taught us: Our Father . . . .

## BLESSING

**Leader:** May the only-begotten Son of God bless us and assist us in all our needs.

**All:** AMEN.

*A sign of peace may be exchanged.*

# ORDINARY TIME I

## FORM 1

*After the Christmas Season to the First Sunday of Lent*

### LIGHT SERVICE

*After lighting the candle(s) on the table:*

**Leader:** Jesus Christ is the light of the world.

**All:** A LIGHT NO DARKNESS CAN OVERCOME.

*or*

**Leader:** Light and peace in Jesus Christ our Lord.

**All:** THANKS BE TO GOD.

*Psalm 27:1, 4, 13-14 (CEV)*

**Solo:** You, LORD, are the light
that keeps me safe.
I am not afraid of anyone.
You protect me,
and I have no fears.

**All:** I ask only one thing, LORD:
Let me live in your house
every day of my life
to see how wonderful you are
and to pray in your temple.

**Solo:** I know that I will live
to see how kind you are.
Trust the LORD!
Be brave and strong
and trust the LORD.

**All:**       Glory to the Father, and to the Son,
          and to the Holy Spirit:
          as it was in the beginning, is now,
          and will be for ever. Amen.

**Leader:**   Let us pray.

          *Pause for silent prayer.*

          Guardian of all,
          in your kindness,
          bless this food.
          Give us strength
          to live as your people,
          both now and for ever.

**All:**       AMEN.


## SHARING OF THE MEAL

*After the dishes are cleared away:*


## SCRIPTURE READING                    *Ephesians 1:3-6*

A reading from the Letter of Paul to the Ephesians

Praise the God and Father of our Lord Jesus Christ for the spiritual blessings that Christ brought us from heaven! Before the world was created, God had Christ choose us to live with him and to be his holy and innocent and loving people. God was kind and decided that Christ would choose us to be God's own adopted children. God was very kind to us because of the Son he dearly loves, and so we should praise God.

**Reader:**   The word of the Lord.

**All:**       THANKS BE TO GOD.

## SILENT REFLECTION

## RESPONSE TO THE READING

**Leader:** Lord, you are kind and full of compassion.

**All:** SLOW TO ANGER, ABOUNDING IN LOVE.

## INTERCESSIONS

**Leader:** Blessed are you, Lord our God. You made us, we belong to you. Hear us as we pray: LORD, GIVE US YOUR SAVING HELP.

• For the Church, that we be built up as living stones into a temple for God in the Spirit:

• For persecuted Christians, that they take courage in the promises of Christ:

• For our civic leaders, that they guide us in creating a more humane world:

• For families, that they embody Christ's call to self-sacrificing love:

• For all who have died *(especially* _____*)*, that they rejoice for ever in the company of the saints:

Let us pray to the Father as Christ himself taught us: Our Father . . . .

## BLESSING

**Leader:** May the peace of Christ live always in our hearts and in our home.

**All:** AMEN.

*A sign of peace may be exchanged.*

# FORM 2

*After the Christmas Season to the First Sunday of Lent*

## LIGHT SERVICE

*After lighting the candle(s) on the table:*

**Leader:** Jesus Christ is the light of the world.

**All:** A LIGHT NO DARKNESS CAN OVERCOME.

*or*

**Leader:** Light and peace in Jesus Christ our Lord.

**All:** THANKS BE TO GOD.

*Psalm 95:1, 3-5, 6-7* (ICEL)

**Solo:** Come, sing with joy to God,
shout to our savior, our rock.
Enter God's presence with praise,
enter with shouting and song.

**All:** A great God is the Lord,
over the gods like a king.
God cradles the depths of the earth,
holds fast the mountain peaks.
God shaped the ocean and owns it,
formed the earth by hand.

**Solo:** Come, bow down and worship,
kneel to the Lord our maker.
This is our God, our shepherd,
we are the flock led with care.

**All:** Glory to the Father, and to the Son,
and to the Holy Spirit:
as it was in the beginning, is now,
and will be for ever. Amen.

**Leader:** Let us pray.

> *Pause for silent prayer.*
>
> Creator of all,
> bless our table
> and make it a sign
> of our belonging to you
> and to each other,
> through Christ our Lord.

**All:** AMEN.

## SHARING OF THE MEAL

*After the dishes are cleared away:*

## SCRIPTURE READING                              *1 John 4:15-18*

A reading from the first letter of John

God stays with everyone who openly says that Jesus is the Son of God. That's how we stay one with God and are sure that God loves us.

God is love. If we keep on loving others, we will stay one in our hearts with God, and he will stay one with us. If we truly love others and live as Christ did in this world, we won't be worried about the day of judgment. A real love for others will chase those worries away.

**Reader:** The word of the Lord.

**All:** THANKS BE TO GOD.

## SILENT REFLECTION

## RESPONSE TO THE READING

**Leader:** Lord, I trust in your merciful love.

**All:** MY HEART REJOICES IN YOUR SAVING HELP.

## INTERCESSIONS

**Leader:** Father, your beloved Son, Jesus Christ, always loved the poor and the lowly. We beg you to send your Spirit to all who stand in great need of your grace, as we pray: LORD, HEAR AND HAVE MERCY.

- For those who suffer pain:

- For those whose minds are disturbed:

- For those forced to live less than the life for which you made them:

- For those who know their guilt and their emptiness, but do not know the love of Christ:

- For those who destroy human life through abortion and euthanasia:

- For those who are aware that they must soon die:

- For all who have died, hoping in the life to come *(especially _____):*

Mindful of all these people, our suffering brothers and sisters, we pray as Jesus taught us: Our Father . . . .

## BLESSING

**Leader:** May Christ bless us with his loving presence and his word of truth.

**All:** AMEN.

*A sign of peace may be exchanged.*

# LENT

## FORM 1

*First, Third, and Fifth Sundays of Lent*

### LIGHT SERVICE

*After lighting the candle(s) on the table:*

**Leader:** Jesus Christ is the light of the world.

**All:** A LIGHT NO DARKNESS CAN OVERCOME.

*or*

**Leader:** Light and peace in Jesus Christ our Lord.

**All:** THANKS BE TO GOD.

*Psalm 51:1-2, 10-11, 12 and 15 (CEV)*

**Solo:** You are kind, God!
Please have pity on me.
You are always merciful.
Please wipe away my sins.
Wash me clean from all
of my sin and guilt.

**All:** Create pure thoughts in me
and make me faithful again.
Don't chase me away from you
or take your Holy Spirit
away from me.

**Solo:**   Make me happy as you did
when you saved me;
make me want to obey!
Help me to speak,
and I will praise you, Lord.

**All:**   Glory to the Father, and to the Son,
and to the Holy Spirit:
as it was in the beginning, is now,
and will be for ever. Amen.

**Leader:**   Let us pray.

*Pause for silent prayer.*

God ever-merciful, bless us and these your gifts.
May our time of prayer and fasting
open us to your work of forgiveness
and free us to rejoice
in the sacrifice of your Son,
Jesus Christ, our Lord.

**All:**   AMEN.

## SHARING OF THE MEAL

*After the dishes are cleared away:*

## SCRIPTURE READING   *Romans 12:1-2, 9-11*

A reading from the Letter of Paul to the Romans

Dear friends, God is good. So I beg you to offer your bodies
to him as a living sacrifice, pure and pleasing. That's the most
sensible way to serve God. Don't be like the people of this
world, but let God change the way you think. Then you will
know how to do everything that is good and pleasing to him.

Be sincere in your love for others. Hate everything that is
evil and hold tight to everything that is good. Love each other
as brothers and sisters and honor others more than you do
yourself. Never give up. Eagerly follow the Holy Spirit and
serve the Lord.

**Reader:** The word of the Lord.

**All:** THANKS BE TO GOD.

### SILENT REFLECTION

### RESPONSE TO THE READING

**Leader:** Lord, you are good and forgiving.

**All:** FULL OF LOVE TO ALL WHO CALL.

### INTERCESSIONS

**Leader:** Jesus Christ suffered for us and left us an example, so that we could follow in his steps. Let us ask him to guide our passage through death to life as we pray: LORD, SHOW US YOUR WAY.

- As we turn away from sin, help us turn to you in penance.

- As we turn away from selfishness and self-deception, help us turn to you by serving others.

- As we turn away from pride and arrogance, help us turn to you in humility.

- As we turn away from anger and hatred, help us turn to you in love.

- As we turn away from works of death, help us turn to you by choosing life.

As we journey with Christ to holy Easter, let us pray as he taught us: Our Father . . . .

### BLESSING

**Leader:** May the only Son of God have mercy on us and help us in all our needs.

**All:** AMEN.

*A sign of peace may be exchanged.*

# FORM 2
*Second and Fourth Sundays of Lent*

## LIGHT SERVICE

*After lighting the candle(s) on the table:*

**Leader:**   Jesus Christ is the light of the world.

**All:**       A LIGHT NO DARKNESS CAN OVERCOME.

*or*

**Leader:**   Light and peace in Jesus Christ our Lord.

**All:**       THANKS BE TO GOD.

*Psalm 130:1-2, 5-6, 6-7, 7-8* (ICEL)

**Solo:**      From the depths I call to you,
Lord, hear my cry.
Catch the sound of my voice
raised up, pleading.

**All:**        I trust in God's word,
I trust in the Lord.
More than sentries for dawn
I watch for the Lord.

**Solo:**      More than sentries for dawn
let Israel watch.

**All:**        The Lord will bring mercy
and grant full pardon.
The Lord will free Israel
from all its sins.

**All:**        Glory to the Father, and to the Son,
and to the Holy Spirit:
as it was in the beginning, is now,
and will be for ever. Amen.

**Leader:** Let us pray.

*Pause for silent prayer.*

God rich in mercy,
send your blessing upon us
and upon our table.
In these Lenten days we wait for you,
full of hope.
As we fast from sin,
let us feast on your mercy
in Jesus Christ, our Lord.

**All:** AMEN.

## SHARING OF THE MEAL

*After the dishes are cleared away:*

## SCRIPTURE READING                    *Ephesians 4:30–5:2*

A reading from the Letter of Paul to the Ephesians

Don't make God's Spirit sad. The Spirit makes you sure that someday you will be free from your sins.

Stop being bitter and angry and mad at others. Don't yell at one another or curse each other or ever be rude. Instead, be kind and merciful, and forgive others, just as God forgave you because of Christ. Do as God does. After all, you are his dear children. Let love be your guide. Christ loved us and offered his life for us as a sacrifice that pleases God.

**Reader:** The word of the Lord.

**All:** THANKS BE TO GOD.

## SILENT REFLECTION

## RESPONSE TO THE READING

**Leader:** Return to the Lord with your whole heart.

**All:**      FOR OUR GOD IS GRACIOUS AND RICH IN KINDNESS.

**INTERCESSIONS**

**Leader:** Lord God, save us in your mercy. By ourselves we are weak and forsaken, but you are a refuge close at hand. Hear us as we pray: HELP US, O LORD.

- To learn your will, so that we may follow the path that leads to life:

- To forgive the daily faults of others, so that we may be worthy of your forgiveness:

- To serve the needs of our sisters and brothers, so that we may all share in the glory of your risen Son:

- To seek justice and lift oppression, so that the weak may find freedom:

- To remember the dead, so that with them we may share eternal life with all the saints:

Let us place all our confidence in God as we pray the Lord's Prayer: Our Father . . . .

**BLESSING**

**Leader:** May the Lord who is faithful guard us from evil and strengthen us in the ways of peace.

**All:**      AMEN.

*A sign of peace may be exchanged.*

# PASSION (PALM) SUNDAY

## LIGHT SERVICE

*After lighting the candle(s) on the table:*

**Leader:** Jesus Christ is the light of the world.

**All:** A LIGHT NO DARKNESS CAN OVERCOME.

*or*

**Leader:** Light and peace in Jesus Christ our Lord.

**All:** THANKS BE TO GOD.

*Psalm 91:1-2, 10-11, 14-15 (CEV)*

**Solo:** Live under the protection
of God Most High
and stay in the shadow
of God All-Powerful.
Then you will say to the LORD,
"You are my fortress,
my place of safety;
you are my God,
and I trust you."

**All:** No terrible disasters
will strike you or your home.
God will command his angels
to protect you
wherever you go.

**Solo:** The LORD says, "If you love me
and truly know who I am,
I will rescue you
and keep you safe.
When you are in trouble,
call out to me.

I will answer and be there
to protect you and honor you."

**All:**     Glory to the Father, and to the Son,
and to the Holy Spirit:
as it was in the beginning, is now,
and will be for ever. Amen.

**Leader:**  Let us pray.

*Pause for silent prayer.*

God, holy and strong,
bless this food
and give us strength
to bring your love
to those in suffering and pain:
*(especially* _____*)*
We ask this through Christ our Lord.

**All:**     AMEN.


## SHARING OF THE MEAL

*After the dishes are cleared away:*


## SCRIPTURE READING                *Hebrews 2:9-11*

A reading from the Letter to the Hebrews

Because of God's kindness, Jesus died for everyone. And now
that Jesus has suffered and died, he is crowned with glory
and honor!

Everything belongs to God, and all things were created by
his power. So God did the right thing when he made Jesus
perfect by suffering, as Jesus led many of God's children
to be saved and to share in his glory. Jesus and the people
he makes holy all belong to the same family. That is why
he is not ashamed to call them his brothers and sisters.

**Reader:**  The word of the Lord.

**All:** THANKS BE TO GOD.

## SILENT REFLECTION

## RESPONSE TO THE READING

**Leader:** Jesus emptied himself and became as we are.

**All:** HIS NAME IS ABOVE ALL OTHER NAMES: JESUS CHRIST IS LORD!.

## INTERCESSIONS

**Leader:** Lord God, you are the source of all life and holiness. With you is our strength and our salvation. Hear us as we pray: LORD, GIVE US LIFE.

- Lord, keep watch over your Church; fill its members with your grace and renew them in your loving kindness.
- Keep watch over the nations; resolve their conflicts and bring them to peace.
- Keep watch over infants and children; feed those who are starving and protect those who suffer abuse.
- Keep watch over all of us; help us to be single-hearted in your service and generous to one another.
- Keep watch over the dying; remove their fear and fulfill their hope to live with you for ever.

Let us pray to the Guardian of our lives as Jesus taught us: Our Father . . . .

## BLESSING

**Leader:** May the Spirit direct our hearts and bodies in the love of God and the patience of Christ.

**All:** AMEN.

*A sign of peace may be exchanged.*

# EASTER SEASON

## EASTER SUNDAY

### LIGHT SERVICE

*After lighting the candle(s) on the table:*

**Leader:** Jesus Christ is the light of the world.
Alleluia, alleluia!

**All:** A LIGHT NO DARKNESS CAN OVERCOME.
ALLELUIA, ALLELUIA!

*or*

**Leader:** Light and peace in Jesus Christ our Lord.
Alleluia, alleluia!

**All:** THANKS BE TO GOD. ALLELUIA, ALLELUIA!

*Psalm 118:1-2, 15-16, 17, 22-23, 24-25, 28-29* (ICEL)

**Solo:** Give thanks, the Lord is good,
God's love is for ever!
Now let Israel say,
"God's love is for ever!"

**All:** Glad songs of victory sound
within the tents of the just.
With right hand raised high,
the Lord strikes with force.

**Solo:** I shall not die but live
to tell the Lord's great deeds.

**All:** The stone the builders rejected
has become the cornerstone.
This is the work of the Lord,
how wonderful in our eyes.

This is the day the Lord made,
let us rejoice and be glad.
Lord, give us the victory!
Lord, grant us success!

**Solo:** I will thank you, my God,
I will praise you highly.
Give thanks, the Lord is good,
God's love is for ever!

**All:** Glory to the Father, and to the Son,
and to the Holy Spirit:
as it was in the beginning, is now,
and will be for ever. Amen. Alleluia!

**Leader:** Let us pray.

*Pause for silent prayer.*

Lord,
on this most holy day,
let your blessing rest upon us
and upon our table.
Fill us with joy and gladness
as we share this time together.
We ask this in Jesus' name.

**All:** AMEN.


## SHARING OF THE MEAL

*After the dishes are cleared away:*


## SCRIPTURE READING                     *Colossians 3:1-4*

A reading from the Letter of Paul to the Colossians

You have been raised to life with Christ. Now set your heart on what is in heaven, where Christ rules at God's right side. Think about what is up there, not about what is here on earth.

You died, which means that your life is hidden with Christ, who sits beside God. Christ gives meaning to your life, and when he appears, you will also appear with him in glory.

**Reader:**　The word of the Lord.

**All:**　THANKS BE TO GOD.

## SILENT REFLECTION

## RESPONSE TO THE READING

**Leader:**　This is the day the Lord has made. Alleluia!

**All:**　LET US REJOICE AND BE GLAD. ALLELUIA!

## INTERCESSIONS

**Leader:**　On this festival day, let us be glad in the testimony of the holy women and the apostles: Jesus has truly risen from the dead! Let us pray that his resurrection will bring new life to the world, as we proclaim: AMEN, ALLELUIA!

• That all Christians, especially those newly reborn through water and the Spirit, will be faithful to their baptism:

• That those who suffer persecution for their witness to the risen Lord will persevere in the freedom of God's children:

• That both the rich and the poor will find strength to live as new people in Christ Jesus:

• That those who suffer from poverty and sickness will know the power flowing from the Lord's resurrection:

- That those who have died in Christ will find eternal life in him *(especially _____)* and see the vision of his glory:

On this first of days, let us glorify the Father as Jesus, victor over death, has taught us: Our Father . . . .

## BLESSING

**Leader:** May the peace of the risen Christ remain with us always.

**All:** AMEN.

*A sign of peace may be exchanged.*

# FORM 1
*Second, Fourth, and Sixth Sundays of Easter*

## LIGHT SERVICE

*After lighting the candle(s) on the table:*

**Leader:** Jesus Christ is the light of the world. Alleluia!

**All:** A LIGHT NO DARKNESS CAN OVERCOME. ALLELUIA!

*or*

**Leader:** Light and peace in Jesus Christ our Lord. Alleluia!

**All:** THANKS BE TO GOD. ALLELUIA!

*Psalm 66:1-3, 4-6, 6-7, 8-9* (ICEL)

**Solo:** All earth, shout with joy to God!
Sing the glory of the Name!
Give glorious praise!
Say, "How awesome your works!"

**All:**     All earth bows before you,
             sings to you, sings to your name.
             Come, see God's wonders,
             tremendous deeds for the people:
             God turned sea into land,
             they crossed the river on foot.

**Solo:**    Let us rejoice then in God,
             who rules for ever with might.
             Bless our God, you peoples,
             loudly sound God's praise,
             who kept our spirits alive
             and our feet from stumbling.

**All:**     Glory to the Father, and to the Son,
             and to the Holy Spirit:
             as it was in the beginning, is now,
             and will be for ever. Amen. Alleluia!

**Leader:**  Let us pray.

             *Pause for silent prayer.*

             God who saves,
             bless this table
             and nurture our faith
             'til it grows into
             praise and worship
             at the glorious coming of Christ Jesus,
             our Lord.

**All:**     AMEN.

## SHARING OF THE MEAL

*After the dishes are cleared away:*

## SCRIPTURE READING                    *1 Peter 1:3-5*

A reading from the First Letter of Peter

Praise God, the Father of our Lord Jesus Christ. God is so
good, and by raising Jesus from death, he has given us new

life and a hope that lives on. God has something stored up for you in heaven, where it will never decay or be ruined or disappear.

You have faith in God, whose power will protect you until the last day. Then he will save you, just as he has always planned to do.

**Reader:**  The word of the Lord.

**All:**  THANKS BE TO GOD.

## SILENT REFLECTION

## RESPONSE TO THE READING

**Leader:**  The Lord has not delivered me to death. Alleluia!

**All:**  I SHALL LIVE AND DECLARE THE WORKS OF THE LORD. ALLELUIA!

## INTERCESSIONS

**Leader:**  By his resurrection, Christ has made known to us the life that lasts for ever. With faith and joy we cry out to him: RISEN SAVIOR, HEAR US!

• By your resurrection, show us today the light of life.

• By your resurrection, speak to us the word of life.

• By your resurrection, nourish us with the bread of life.

• By your resurrection, pour out on us the Spirit of life.

• By your resurrection, prepare for us the crown of life.

• By your resurrection, enroll in the book of life those who have died *(especially* _____*),* and be for them the fullness of life.

In the words Jesus gave us, let us pray to share the life of God's reign: Our Father . . . .

**BLESSING**

**Leader:**  May the resurrection of Jesus be to us a source of blessing and life, both now and for ever.

**All:**  AMEN.

*A sign of peace may be exchanged.*

# FORM 2

*Third, Fifth, and Seventh Sundays of Easter*

## LIGHT SERVICE

*After lighting the candle(s) on the table:*

**Leader:**  Jesus Christ is the light of the world. Alleluia!

**All:**  A LIGHT NO DARKNESS CAN OVERCOME. ALLELUIA!

*or*

**Leader:**  Light and peace in Jesus Christ our Lord. Alleluia!

**All:**  THANKS BE TO GOD. ALLELUIA!

*Psalm 118:1-2, 15-16, 17, 22-23, 24-25, 28-29* (ICEL)

**Solo:**  Give thanks, the Lord is good,
God's love is for ever!
Now let Israel say,
"God's love is for ever!"

**All:**  Glad songs of victory sound
within the tents of the just.
With right hand raised high,
the Lord strikes with force.

**Solo:**  I shall not die but live
to tell the Lord's great deeds.

**All:** The stone the builders rejected
has become the cornerstone.
This is the work of the Lord,
how wonderful in our eyes.

This is the day the Lord made,
let us rejoice and be glad.
Lord, give us the victory!
Lord, grant us success!

**Solo:** I will thank you, my God,
I will praise you highly.
Give thanks, the Lord is good,
God's love is for ever!

**All:** Glory to the Father, and to the Son,
and to the Holy Spirit:
as it was in the beginning, is now,
and will be for ever. Amen. Alleluia!

**Leader:** Let us pray.

*Pause for silent prayer.*

Victorious God,
we put our faith in you
as Jesus did,
and thank you for keeping us safe.
In this most holy season,
let your blessing rest upon us
and upon our table.
We ask this in Jesus' name.

**All:** AMEN.

## SHARING OF THE MEAL

*After the dishes are cleared away:*

## SCRIPTURE READING                    *Revelation 1:5-6*

A reading from the Book of Revelation

May kindness and peace be yours from Jesus Christ, the faithful witness. Jesus was the first to conquer death, and he is the ruler of all earthly kings. Christ loves us, and by his blood he set us free from our sins. He lets us rule as kings and serve God his Father as priests. To him be glory and power forever and ever! Amen.

**Reader:** The word of the Lord.

**All:** THANKS BE TO GOD.

## SILENT REFLECTION

## RESPONSE TO THE READING

**Leader:** Seek the Son of Man no more among the dead. Alleluia!

**All:** HE HAS BROKEN THE BONDS OF DEATH. ALLELUIA!

## INTERCESSIONS

**Leader:** Christ has been raised, the first-born from the dead. Let us rejoice in his triumph over sin and death as we pray: KING OF GLORY, HEAR OUR PRAYER.

• For renewed commitment to your service:

• For the peace which comes only from you:

• For an end to the destruction of human life throughout the world:

• For greater generosity toward the poor:

• For an end to discrimination and prejudice:

• For compassion toward the needs of the sick and disabled:

• For your protection this day *(night)*:

• For your mercy at the moment of our death:

Remembering God's love and care for us, let us pray in the words of Jesus our brother: Our Father . . . .

## BLESSING

**Leader:**  May the risen Christ grant us a share of his life and glory, both now and for ever.

**All:**  AMEN.

*A sign of peace may be exchanged.*

# PENTECOST SUNDAY

## LIGHT SERVICE

*After lighting the candle(s) on the table:*

**Leader:**  Jesus Christ is the light of the world.
Alleluia, alleluia!

**All:**  A LIGHT NO DARKNESS CAN OVERCOME.
ALLELUIA, ALLELUIA!

*or*

**Leader:**  Light and peace in Jesus Christ our Lord.
Alleluia, alleluia!

**All:**  THANKS BE TO GOD. ALLELUIA, ALLELUIA!

*Psalm 104:1abc and 24, 30-31 (CEV)*

**Solo:**  I praise you, LORD God,
with all my heart.
You are glorious and majestic.
Our LORD, by your wisdom
you made so many things;
the whole earth is covered
with your living creatures.

**All:**     You created all of them
             by your Spirit,
             and you give new life
             to the earth.
             Our LORD, we pray
             that your glory will last for ever
             and that you will be pleased
             with what you have done.

**All:**     Glory to the Father, and to the Son,
             and to the Holy Spirit:
             as it was in the beginning, is now,
             and will be for ever. Amen. Alleluia!

**Leader:**  Let us pray.

             *Pause for silent prayer.*

             Lord Jesus,
             the fullness of your love
             fills the universe in all its parts.
             Send your Spirit
             to bless this table
             and fill us with your life,
             for ever and ever.

**All:**     AMEN.


## SHARING OF THE MEAL

*After the dishes are cleared away:*


## SCRIPTURE READING                 *Galatians 5:22-25*

A reading from the Letter of Paul to the Galatians

God's Spirit makes us loving, happy, peaceful, patient, kind, good, faithful, gentle, and self-controlled. There is no law against behaving in any of these ways. And because we belong to Christ, we have killed our selfish feelings and desires.

God's Spirit has given us life, and so we should follow the Spirit.

**Reader:** The word of the Lord.

**All:** THANKS BE TO GOD.

## SILENT REFLECTION

## RESPONSE TO THE READING

**Leader:** Come, Holy Spirit, fill the hearts of your faithful. Alleluia!

**All:** AND KINDLE IN THEM THE FIRE OF YOUR LOVE. ALLELUIA!

## INTERCESSIONS

**Leader:** Lord Jesus Christ, you were raised to the right hand of the Father and sent the Holy Spirit upon your disciples. Like them, we trust in your promises and cry out with one voice: AMEN, ALLELUIA!

- You promised the life-giving Spirit to all who thirst. By your Spirit, fill us with the holiness for which we long.

- You promised that the Spirit would teach us all things. By your Spirit, deepen our faith in your care for us.

- You promised to send the Spirit of truth. By your Spirit, empower us to be your faithful witnesses.

- You promised that the Spirit would remain in your Church until the final day. By your Spirit, strengthen persecuted Christians with courage and perseverance.

- You promised that the Spirit would give life. By your Spirit, raise up the dead *(especially _____ )* and let them share your glory.

Let us pray in Spirit and truth the prayer Jesus taught us:
Our Father . . . .

## BLESSING

**Leader:**   May the Holy Spirit of God always fill our hearts
with love.

**All:**   AMEN.

*A sign of peace may be exchanged.*

# ORDINARY TIME II

## FORM 1

*Pentecost to September 1*

### LIGHT SERVICE

*After lighting the candle(s) on the table:*

**Leader:** Jesus Christ is the light of the world.

**All:** A LIGHT NO DARKNESS CAN OVERCOME.

*or*

**Leader:** Light and peace in Jesus Christ our Lord.

**All:** THANKS BE TO GOD.

*Psalm 34:1-2, 4-5, 6-7, 8-9, 10-11* (ICEL)

**Solo:** I will never stop thanking God,
with constant words of praise.
My soul will boast of God;
the poor will hear me and be glad.

**All:** Join me in praising the Lord,
together tell of God's name.
I asked and the Lord responded,
freed me from all my fears.

**Solo:** Turn to God, be bright with joy;
you shall never be let down.
I begged and God heard,
took my burdens from me.

**All:**      God's angel defends the faithful,
              guards them on every side.
              Drink in the richness of God,
              enjoy the strength of the Lord.

**Solo:**     Live in awe of God, you saints:
              you will want for nothing.
              Even if lions go hungry,
              those seeking God are fed.

**All:**      Glory to the Father, and to the Son,
              and to the Holy Spirit:
              as it was in the beginning, is now,
              and will be for ever. Amen.

**Leader:**   Let us pray.

              *Pause for silent prayer.*

              Ever-faithful God,
              bless the food we are about to eat
              and unite us in mind and heart
              to your Son,
              Jesus Christ, the Lord.

**All:**      AMEN.


## SHARING OF THE MEAL

*After the dishes are cleared away:*


## SCRIPTURE READING             *1 Corinthians 13:4-8*

A reading from the First Letter of Paul to the Corinthians

Love is kind and patient, never jealous, boastful, proud, or rude. Love isn't selfish, or quick-tempered. It doesn't keep a record of wrongs that others do. Love rejoices in the truth, but not in evil. Love is always supportive, loyal, hopeful, and trusting. Love never fails.

**Reader:** The word of the Lord.

**All:** THANKS BE TO GOD.

## SILENT REFLECTION

## RESPONSE TO THE READING

**Leader:** There are three things that last:
faith, hope, and love.

**All:** AND THE GREATEST OF THESE IS LOVE.

## INTERCESSIONS

**Leader:** Father, we thank you for the great lights of sun
and moon, which illumine our path by day and
night, and above all for Jesus Christ, the true light
which enlightens all who come into the world. In
his name we ask you: LORD, SHOW US YOUR
LOVE.

- Pour the graces of this Sunday into the daily lives of all
  who celebrate Christ's resurrection.

- Lead all peoples estranged by hatred and war to be recon-
  ciled in the peace of your Son.

- Open our eyes to the wonders of your creation, and deepen
  our respect for the life you have given us.

- Brighten the lives of the sick, aged, and infirm, and help
  them find strength in sharing the suffering of Christ.

- Scatter the darkness of sin and error in our lives, and forgive our offenses against one another.

- Raise up all who have died *(especially* _____ *)* and admit
  them to the light of eternal day.

And now, Father, we pray the prayer Jesus gave us:
Our Father . . . .

**BLESSING**

**Leader:** May God make us steadfast in faith, joyful in hope, and untiring in love all the days of our life.

**All:** AMEN.

*A sign of peace may be exchanged.*

# FORM 2
*Pentecost to September 1*

## LIGHT SERVICE

*After lighting the candle(s) on the table:*

**Leader:** Jesus Christ is the light of the world.

**All:** A LIGHT NO DARKNESS CAN OVERCOME.

*or*

**Leader:** Light and peace in Jesus Christ our Lord.

**All:** THANKS BE TO GOD.

*Psalm 63:1, 2-3, 4-5, 7-8 (CEV)*

**Solo:** You are my God, I worship you.
In my heart, I long for you,
as I would long for a stream
in a scorching desert.

**All:** I have seen your power
and your glory
in the place of worship.
Your love means more
than life to me,
and I praise you.

**Solo:** As long as I live,
I will pray to you.
I will sing joyful praises
and be filled with excitement
like a guest at a banquet.

**All:** You have helped me,
and I sing happy songs
in the shadow of your wings.
I stay close to you,
and your powerful arm
supports me.

**All:** Glory to the Father, and to the Son,
and to the Holy Spirit:
as it was in the beginning, is now,
and will be for ever. Amen.

**Leader:** Let us pray.

*Pause for silent prayer.*

All-merciful God,
send your life-giving Spirit
on our household
and on all dear to us,
and bless this table
as we join together and say:

**All:** AMEN.

## SHARING OF THE MEAL

*After the dishes are cleared away:*

## SCRIPTURE READING          *Ephesians 3:16-17, 19*

A reading from the Letter of Paul to the Ephesians

God is wonderful and glorious. I pray that his Spirit will make you become strong followers and that Christ will live in your hearts because of your faith. Stand firm and be deeply rooted in his love. I want you to know all about Christ's love, although it is too wonderful to be measured. Then your lives will be filled with all that God is.

**Reader:**  The word of the Lord.

**All:**  THANKS BE TO GOD.

## SILENT REFLECTION

## RESPONSE TO THE READING

**Leader:**  Give thanks to the Lord, for the Lord is good.

**All:**  GOD'S LOVE IS EVERLASTING.

## INTERCESSIONS

**Leader:**  Lord God, all that we are we owe to you. For you have created and redeemed us, and help us to live as your people. In your kindness, listen as we pray: LORD, HEAR AND HAVE MERCY.

• Free Christians from every habit of thought that stands against the gospel of Jesus.

• Never allow us to forget those who live under the shadow of poverty, injustice, or war.

• Strengthen the spirit of all who care for the dying and the mentally ill.

• Reconcile the members of broken families and heal all their wounds.

• Bless our relatives and friends with the gift of your peace.

• Comfort those troubled with sickness, and support those in terror of death.

Let us pray as our Lord himself has taught us:
Our Father . . . .

**BLESSING**

**Leader:** May God be with us in sorrow and in joy, and give us lasting light and peace.

**All:** AMEN.

*A sign of peace may be exchanged.*

# ORDINARY TIME III

## FORM 1
*September 1 to Advent*

**LIGHT SERVICE**

*After lighting the candle(s) on the table:*

**Leader:** Jesus Christ is the light of the world.

**All:** A LIGHT NO DARKNESS CAN OVERCOME.

*or*

**Leader:** Light and peace in Jesus Christ our Lord.

**All:** THANKS BE TO GOD.

*Psalm 100:1-2, 3, 5* (ICEL)

**Solo:** Shout joy to the Lord, all earth,
serve the Lord with gladness,
enter God's presence with joy!

**All:** Know that the Lord is God,
our maker to whom we belong,
our shepherd, and we the flock.

**Solo:** Indeed the Lord is good!
God's love is for ever,
faithful from age to age.

**All:** Glory to the Father, and to the Son,
and to the Holy Spirit:
as it was in the beginning, is now,
and will be for ever. Amen.

**Leader:** Let us pray.

> *Pause for silent prayer.*

> Lord of the harvest,
> bless this food
> which comes to us in your faithful love.
> Let your goodness be for us and all people
> the source of abundant life and health,
> both now and for ever.

**All:** AMEN.


## SHARING OF THE MEAL

*After the dishes are cleared away:*


## SCRIPTURE READING · Philippians 2:2-4, 14-15

A reading from the Letter of Paul to the Philippians

Christ encourages you, and his love comforts you. God's Spirit unites you, and you are concerned for others. Now make me completely happy! Live in harmony by showing love for each other. Be united in what you think, as if you were only one person. Don't be jealous or proud, but be humble and consider others more important than yourselves. Care about them as much as you care about yourselves and think the same way that Jesus Christ did.

**Reader:** The word of the Lord.

**All:** THANKS BE TO GOD.


## SILENT REFLECTION

## RESPONSE TO THE READING

**Leader:** I give you a new commandment, says the Lord:

**All:** LOVE ONE ANOTHER AS I HAVE LOVED YOU.

## INTERCESSIONS

**Leader:**  Lord God, you have called us to bear witness to a new heaven and a new earth, in the midst of a world that still bears the mark of sin and death. Hear us now, as we pray: HAVE MERCY ON YOUR PEOPLE, LORD.

• For the leaders of the Church:

• For those who govern and protect us:

• For people who improve the quality of human life:

• For all who are hungry, homeless, or exploited by the powerful of this world:

• For spouses and children who are abused:

• For our relatives and friends who are ill *(especially _____ ):*

• For those who are dying with no one to comfort them:

Let us pray as our Lord Jesus Christ has taught us:
Our Father . . . .


## BLESSING

**Leader:**  May God direct our steps and show us how to walk in love and peace.

**All:**  AMEN.

*A sign of peace may be exchanged.*

# FORM 2
*September 1 to Advent*

## LIGHT SERVICE

*After lighting the candle(s) on the table:*

**Leader:**  Jesus Christ is the light of the world.

**All:**  A LIGHT NO DARKNESS CAN OVERCOME.

*or*

**Leader:**  Light and peace in Jesus Christ our Lord.

**All:**  THANKS BE TO GOD.

*Psalm 145:1-2, 8-9, 10-11 (CEV)*

**Solo:**  I will praise you,
my God and King,
and always honor your name.
I will praise you each day
and always honor your name.

**All:**  You are merciful, LORD!
You are kind and patient
and always loving.
You are good to everyone,
and you take care
of all your creation.

**Solo:**  All creation will thank you,
and your loyal people
will praise you.
They will tell about
your marvelous kingdom
and your power.

**All:**  Glory to the Father, and to the Son,
and to the Holy Spirit:
as it was in the beginning, is now,
and will be for ever. Amen.

**Leader:**  Let us pray.

> *Pause for silent prayer.*

> Ruler of nature,
> bless the food we are about to eat,
> and bless those whose toil has produced it
> for our enjoyment.
> Let us see your gracious hand
> in all your works,
> so that we may rejoice in your goodness
> all our days,
> both now and for ever.

**All:**      AMEN.


## SHARING OF THE MEAL

*After the dishes are cleared away:*


## SCRIPTURE READING                    *Ephesians 1:17-18*

A reading from the Letter of Paul to the Ephesians

I ask the glorious Father and God of our Lord Jesus Christ to give you his Spirit. The Spirit will make you wise and let you understand what it means to know God. My prayer is that light will flood your hearts and that you will understand the hope that was given to you when God chose you. Then you will discover the glorious blessings that will be yours together with all of God's people.

**Reader:**  The word of the Lord.

**All:**      THANKS BE TO GOD.


## SILENT REFLECTION


## RESPONSE TO THE READING

**Leader:**  It is you, O Lord, who are my hope.

**All:**     MY TRUST, O LORD, SINCE MY YOUTH.

## INTERCESSIONS

**Leader:** Lord God, your love embraces all peoples and your kindness knows no limit. We rejoice to place our hope in you, our mighty God, as we pray: LORD, HEAR AND GIVE ANSWER.

• Teach us to live our lives gently with others, and to trust that you will never be far from us.

• Fill our lawmakers with a deep love for life, truth, and justice.

• Help all refugees to find a place of rest and a time of peace.

• Pour out the grace of mutual love and trust on married couples and on those preparing for marriage.

• Grant a share in the risen life of your Son to all who have died *(especially _____).*

Let us pray the prayer which the Lord Jesus gave us:
Our Father . . . .

## BLESSING

**Leader:** May God the Father and the Lord Jesus Christ grant peace, love, and faith to all of us.

**All:**     AMEN.

*A sign of peace may be exchanged.*